infographics
HOW IT WORKS

T0022634

MACHINES AND MOTORS

JON RICHARDS AND ED SIMKINS

Gareth Stevens
PUBLISHING

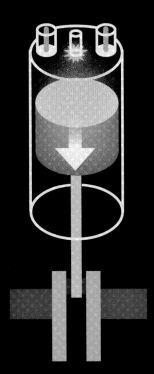

Please visit our website,
www.garethstevens.com.
For a free color catalog of all our
high-quality books, call toll free
1-800-542-2595 or fax 1-877-542-2596.

CATALOGING-IN-PUBLICATION DATA

Names: Richards, Jon. | Simkins, Ed.
  Title: Machines and motors / Jon Richards
  and Ed Simkins.
Description: New York : Gareth Stevens
  Publishing, 2018. | Series: Infographics:
  how it works | Includes index.
Identifiers: ISBN 9781538213520 (pbk.) |
  ISBN 9781538213544 (library bound) |
  ISBN 9781538213537 (6 pack)
Subjects: LCSH: Vehicles--Juvenile
  literature. | Machinery--Juvenile
  literature.
Classification: LCC TL147.R47 2018 |
  DDC 629.04'6--dc23

Published in 2018 by
Gareth Stevens Publishing
111 East 14th Street, Suite 349
New York, NY 10003

Copyright © 2018 Wayland, a division
of Hachette Children's Group

Editor: Liza Miller
Produced by Tall Tree Ltd
Editor: Jon Richards
Designer: Ed Simkins

Printed in China

CPSIA compliance information: Batch CW18GS:
For further information contact Gareth Stevens,
New York, New York at 1-800-542-2595.

CONTENTS

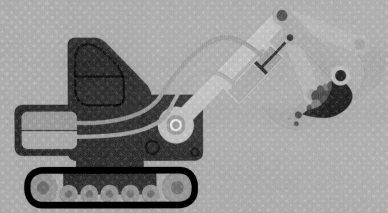

MAKING LIFE EASIER

Machines and motors are designed to make work easier, whether it's lifting a huge load or carrying hundreds of people high in the air over thousands of miles (km). This book will show you how some of these devices work.

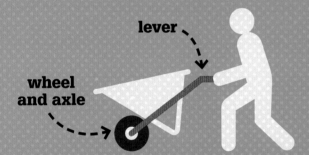

lever

wheel and axle

SIMPLE MACHINES

Scientists say that there are six simple machines. In this book, you will come across devices and objects that use these simple machines to carry out work.

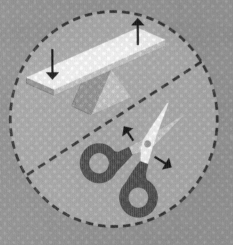

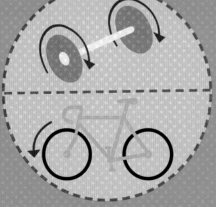

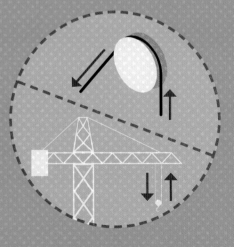

Lever
A lever uses a rod or beam that rotates around a pivot to move a load. Levers can be found on wheelbarrows and scissors.

Wheel and axle
This machine uses a wheel that rotates around an axle in its center. Wheels and axles can be found on vehicles such as bicycles, cars, and trucks.

Pulley
Pulleys use a wheel and an axle to change the direction of a force that is being applied through a rope or a belt. They can be found on cranes.

MOTORS

A motor, or engine, changes one form of energy into movement. A car engine uses chemical energy stored in gasoline. The engine burns the gasoline. to move pistons and turn wheels.

Inclined plane
This machine uses a sloped surface to raise an object. Inclined planes are found on ramps and slides.

Wedge
A wedge is a triangular tool with one thin end and one thick end. Wedges are found on axes and knives.

Screw
Screws have an inclined plane wrapped around a rod. They change rotational movement into horizontal movement.

HOW TO MAKE A
BICYCLE GO

Pedaling a bike can be hard work, especially if you choose the wrong gear. Bicycles have different gears to suit different conditions, such as riding up a steep hill, along a flat road, or over rough ground.

The very first bikes didn't use pedals and gears. Instead, riders pushed the bikes along with their feet.

❶ CHAIN

The chain wheel and the rear wheel of a bicycle are linked by a chain, so that when the pedals turn, the rear wheel turns as well.

❷ LOW GEAR

When using a low gear, the chain runs around the largest of the cogs attached to the rear wheel. For every whole turn of the chain wheel, the rear wheel turns a small amount. This makes the bike easier to move when stationary, going over rough ground, or up a steep hill, but the rider won't be able to go very fast.

low gear/ large cog

pedals

chain wheel

chain

rear wheel

TRY THIS...

Try cycling up a hill using a low gear, and then try cycling up it again in a high gear. Which is easier?

Fred Rompelberg of the Netherlands holds the record for the fastest speed on a bicycle. Riding behind a dragster fitted with a windshield to help him, he managed a speed of 167 miles per hour (269 km/h)!

❸ SHIFT UP

Changing up to a higher gear moves the chain to one of the smaller rear cogs.

high gear/small cog

❹ HIGH GEAR

This time, for every whole turn the chain wheel makes, the rear wheel turns a large amount. This makes the bike harder to move when stationary, but it will go faster.

HOW TO STOP A BICYCLE

When you stop pedaling, your bike's speed will slow (unless you're riding down a hill). This is caused by friction between the tires and the road. However, if you want to stop suddenly, then you need to increase the friction a little.

brake cable

brake handle

❶ BRAKES

To slow down a bike, you squeeze the brake handles. These are connected to the brakes by long cables.

The BLOODHOUND Project is attempting to break the world land speed record. Their rocket-powered Bloodhound SSC car will use air brakes, parachutes, and steel brakes to slow down from 1,000 miles per hour (1,609 km/h) to a stop.

Rub your finger against a tabletop and you may find that it gets warmer. This heat is caused by friction. Brake pads and discs get hot in the same way.

❷ SQUEEZE

As the brake handles are squeezed, they pull on the cables. The cables pull on brake calipers by each wheel.

❸ FRICTION

The calipers squeeze rubber brake pads against the rim of the wheel, or a brake disc that is connected to the wheel.

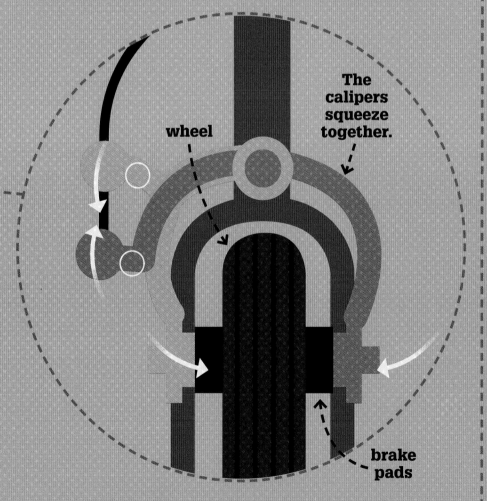

wheel

The calipers squeeze together.

brake pads

parachute

wires

There are many other ways of slowing down people and vehicles. Some racing cars and skydivers use parachutes to trap air and slow their movement. Fighter planes landing on an aircraft carrier have long hooks that catch on wires across the deck to bring them to a stop.

❹ SLOW

The brakes cause an increase in friction that slows down the wheel and the bike with it.

HOW A CRANE LIFTS

Towering above a city's street, cranes lift loads into the air and carry them to high or difficult-to-reach places. They do this by using long cables that are wound around systems of wheels called pulleys. Pulleys can make lifting loads easier.

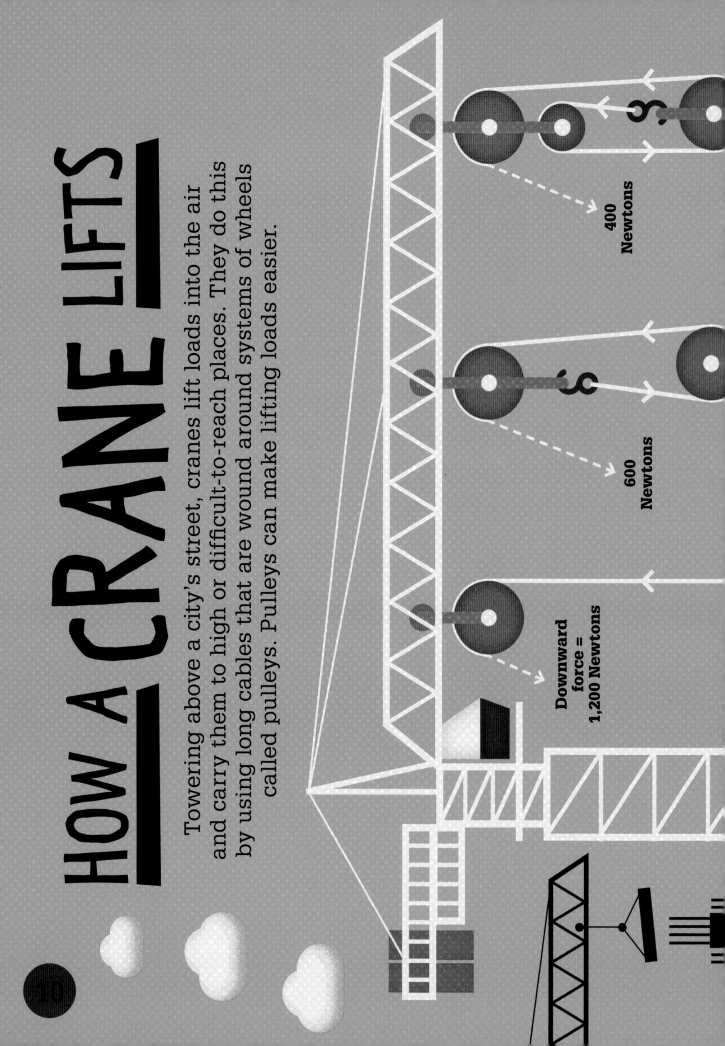

400 Newtons

600 Newtons

Downward force = 1,200 Newtons

10

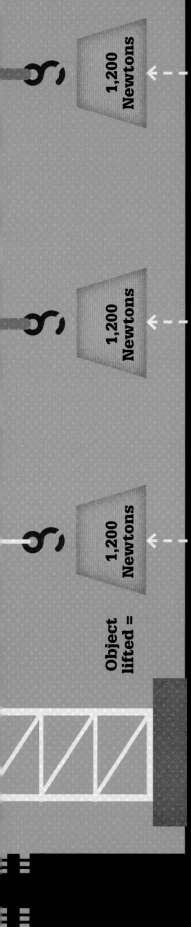

| Object lifted = | 1,200 Newtons | 1,200 Newtons | 1,200 Newtons |

The Taisun crane in China can lift loads weighing more than 22,000 tons (20,000 metric tons) — that's twice the weight of the Eiffel Tower!

❶ PULLEY

A pulley redirects a force so that if a cable is pulled down, the downward force actually lifts an object. A pulley with a single wheel will need a force equal to the weight of the object to lift it off the ground.

❷ TWO WHEELS

Adding a second wheel will halve the amount of force needed. So if the object has a weight of 1,200 Newtons, you will only have to use a force of 600 Newtons. However, you will have to pull the cable twice the distance.

❸ THIRD WHEEL

Adding a third wheel means you only have to use a third of the force. So, if the object has a weight of 1,200 Newtons, you will only have to use a force of 400 Newtons. But you will have to pull the cable three times the distance.

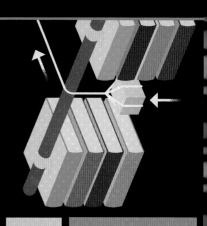

TRY THIS...

Set up a simple pulley by passing a length of string over a dowel that's taped on top of two piles of books. Tie one length of the string to an object and pull on the other end to lift the object. Try raising other objects, some light and some heavy.

HOW AN EXCAVATOR DIGS

On a construction site, excavators and other construction machines gouge out chunks of rocks and earth, and lift the load into dump trucks. To do this they use a system of pipes, pistons, and fluids called hydraulics.

1 EXTENDING

To extend a hydraulic piston, fluid is pumped into one end. When a fluid is pushed from one end of a pipe, it transmits the force to the other end of the pipe.

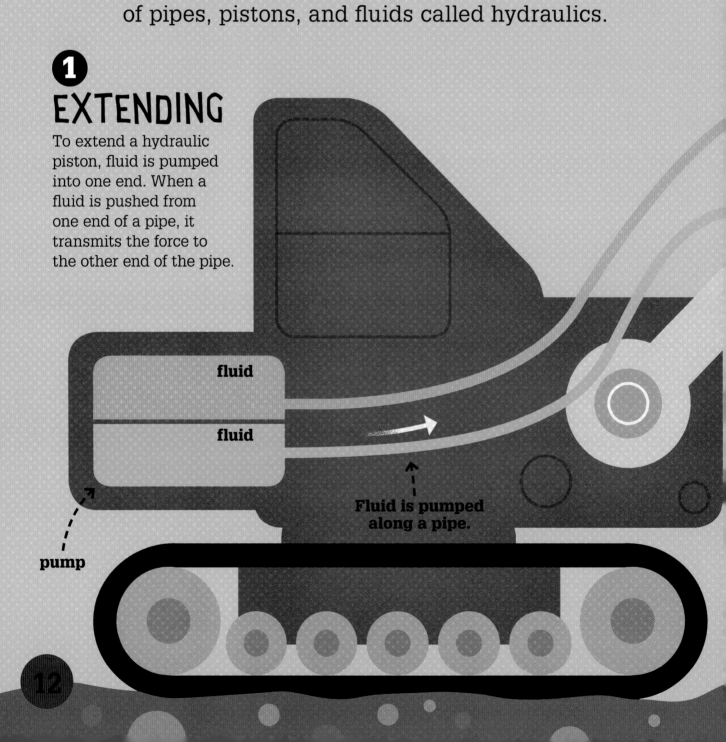

fluid

fluid

pump

Fluid is pumped along a pipe.

❷ PUSHING

As more fluid is pumped in, the pressure increases and pushes on the piston at the other end of the cylinder. The fluid pushes the piston out of the cylinder.

TRY THIS...

The world's largest dump truck can carry a load of 550 tons (500 metric tons). If an excavator can lift 28 tons, how many times must it unload to fill the dump truck?

fluid

hydraulic piston

cylinder

The excavator's arm extends out.

❸ MOVING

As the piston moves out, it pushes on the excavator's arm, extending it so that the excavator reaches out.

❹ BACK AGAIN

To move the arm in the other direction, fluid is let out of the cylinder and the piston slides back. At the same time, fluid is pumped into the other end of the cylinder, pushing the arm in the other direction.

The piston moves back.

HOW A CAR GOES

Under the hood of a car, an engine burns fuel to make the force that turns the wheels. This force is produced by many tiny explosions per second in a process called the four-stroke cycle.

The valve opens.

spark plug

air and fuel

piston

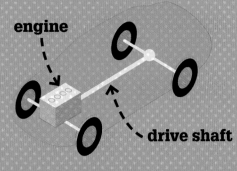

engine

drive shaft

rod

cylinder

❶ FIRST STROKE

In the first stage, the piston drops and valves at the top of the cylinders open to let in both air and fuel. These mix together inside the cylinder.

❷ SECOND STROKE

The piston starts to rise, squeezing the mixture of fuel and air, increasing the pressure. When the piston reaches its highest point, the spark plug at the top of the cylinder produces a spark, igniting the air and fuel mixture.

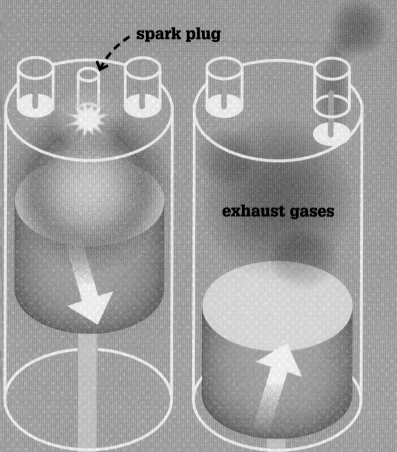

spark plug

exhaust gases

⑤ AND REPEAT

The cycle repeats, producing an up-and-down movement in the engine's pistons. These are connected to a rod called the crankshaft, and this up-and-down movement is translated into a spinning movement. Each full cycle spins the crankshaft twice, creating two revolutions.

⑥ TRANSMITTING

This spinning movement is transferred to the car's wheels through the gears and the drive shaft. The drive shaft carries the force to the wheels and spins them around.

crankshaft

③ THIRD STROKE

This produces a mini-explosion, which pushes the piston back down the cylinder.

④ FOURTH STROKE

The piston starts to rise again. Another valve at the top of the cylinder opens and the exhaust gases are pushed out.

TRY THIS...

The next time you are in a car, see if it has a rev, or revolutions, counter. This shows how quickly the engine is spinning (usually in thousands of revolutions per second).

HOW TO MAKE ELECTRICITY USING WIND POWER

When you flick a light switch, you expect the light to turn on. The switch completes a circuit, allowing electricity to flow to the bulb and the light to glow. Wind turbines produce power for our homes by converting the energy of moving air into electricity.

❶ LONG BLADES

As the wind blows over the long blades of the turbine, they start to spin around.

blade

wind

wind

wind

❷ SPINNING

The shaft of the blades is connected to a coil of wire, which also spins.

wire coil

shaft

magnet

❸ MAGNETS

The coil sits inside a magnetic field, and as the coil spins, it produces an electric current.

Can you think of other methods to spin a turbine? How are turbines sent spinning in a hydroelectric dam?

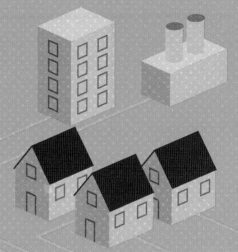

❺ HOME

Further transformers change the voltage again so it is safe to use in our homes.

❹ CURRENT

The electric current passes to a transformer. This produces the correct voltage to send the electricity along power lines.

electric current

power lines

transformer

A single wind turbine capable of producing 6 megawatts of electricity could supply enough power for about 5,500 homes.

HOW TO DRY YOUR HAIR

Inside a hair dryer is a small electric motor that turns a fan. There is also a heating element that warms the blown air to dry your hair. So what happens when you turn it on?

fan

switch

electric motor

❶ MAKING A CIRCUIT

When the switch is flicked, a circuit is completed and electricity flows through the motor.

❷ SPINNING

Inside the motor is a coil of wire sitting inside a magnetic field. As electricity flows through the coil, it starts to spin around.

magnet

wire coil

wire carrying electric current

❸ FAN

The wire coil is attached to a fan that blows air as it spins.

warm air

heating element

4 HOT AIR

At the same time, electricity flows through a special wire called a heating element, which starts to heat up.

Electric motors aren't just used in household objects. They can also be used to power cars and even trains.

5 DRYING

The warm element heats up air as it is blown out of the dryer. This hot air speeds up the rate at which water evaporates from wet hair, drying it quickly.

TRY THIS...

Go around your school and make a list of everything that uses an electric motor. Does your school have automatic doors and gates that can open themselves? Are there fans in classrooms and offices? Do you think all these objects need motors? What other things could use an electric motor?

HOW TO HARVEST A CROP

Gathering a crop requires some large machines called combine harvesters. These cut and collect the plants and then separate the grain from the unwanted stalks and chaff.

1 CUTTER

The rotating reel guides the plants to the harvester's cutter bar, which cuts the plants.

2 PUSHING

A rotating auger pushes the cut plants back on to a conveyor, which pulls them into the harvester.

threshing drum

rotating auger

crops

rotating reel

cutter bar

fan

If a wheat field covering an area of 37 acres contains 51 tons of grain, how many combine harvesters, each with a collection rate of 3 tons per day, would it take to harvest the whole field in a single day?

The largest combine harvesters can collect up to 5 tons (5 metric tons) of wheat grain in a day's work.

grain

❸ THRESHING

Inside the threshing drum, grain and chaff are separated from the straw. Most of the grain and chaff fall through holes in the threshing drum.

❹ SIEVING

The straw passes back over a series of walkers, through which any grain trapped in the straw falls. The straw then passes out of the back of the harvester.

❺ GRAIN

Any unwanted chaff is then blown off by fans, because it is so light. This leaves the grain behind, which can then be unloaded into a trailer being pulled by a tractor.

straw and chaff

walkers   grain tank

HOW TO DIG A TUNNEL

Deep below the ground, long tunnel-boring machines (TBMs) dig out tunnels that run under cities, through mountains, and even beneath the sea. They use enormous, toothed wheels to cut through the rock, and massive pipes to remove the debris.

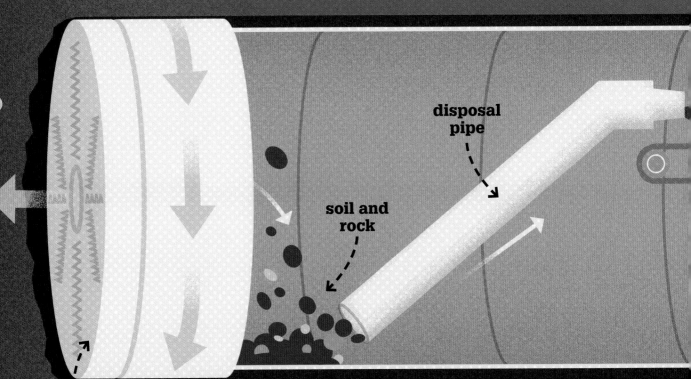

disposal pipe

soil and rock

cutterhead

1 GOUGING

At the front of the TBM is a huge disc called the cutterhead, which is covered in large, sharp teeth. As this spins around, it gouges out the rock and soil in front of the TBM.

2 DISPOSAL

The soil is guided through holes in the cutterhead. Water and chemicals are added to turn this soil into a paste called slurry. The slurry travels to the back of the TBM for disposal.

slurry

The waste is carried away.

curved concrete

3 LINING

As the TBM gradually grinds up the rock and soil, it creeps forwards. Huge, curved pieces of concrete are put in place behind it to line the tunnel wall and stop it from collapsing.

Each concrete lining ring can weigh 180 tons (163 metric tons) — more than 40 African elephants.

HOW A
PLANE FLIES

Planes fly by producing a force called lift.
To create this force, they need to have air
flowing over wings that have a special
shape called an aerofoil section.

thrust

1 THRUST

In order to get air flowing
over the wings, the plane
needs to be moving
forwards. To do this,
it needs to produce
forward thrust,
which it can do
using a propeller
or a jet engine.

lift

faster
air

2 WING

The special shape of
the wing means
that air flowing over
it moves faster and
has a lower pressure
than air flowing
under the wing. This
pressure difference
pushes the wing up.

wing

slower
air

TRY THIS...

See how the shape of a wing creates lift. Hold a thin, small sheet of paper against your chin just beneath your lips. Now blow across the upper surface of the sheet and watch as the sheet rises.

4 LIFT

Together, these forces on the wing produce lift, which keeps the plane in the air.

lift

3 ATTACK

The wing is also angled upwards slightly. This angle is called the angle of attack and it deflects air downwards, which also pushes up on the wing.

angle of attack

jet engine

air flow

wing

HOW A SUBMARINE DIVES

Submarines can dive below the water and rise to the surface again. They do so by pumping air into and out of special tanks. This adjusts the way they float, or their buoyancy.

➊ BUOYANCY

When a submarine is floating at one level, including on the surface, it is said to have neutral buoyancy.

hydroplanes

Air is let out.

submarine dives

air tank

ballast tank

Water is let in.

➋ DIVE, DIVE!

In order to dive, it lets air out of its ballast tanks and fills them with water. This makes the whole submarine heavier than the water around it, so it sinks down.

➌ FINS

It also turns special fins called hydroplanes. These push the nose of the submarine down.

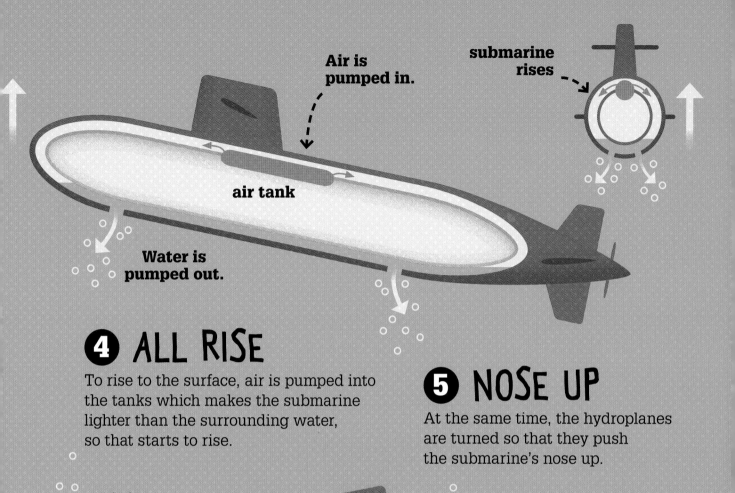

Air is pumped in.

submarine rises

air tank

Water is pumped out.

❹ ALL RISE

To rise to the surface, air is pumped into the tanks which makes the submarine lighter than the surrounding water, so that starts to rise.

❺ NOSE UP

At the same time, the hydroplanes are turned so that they push the submarine's nose up.

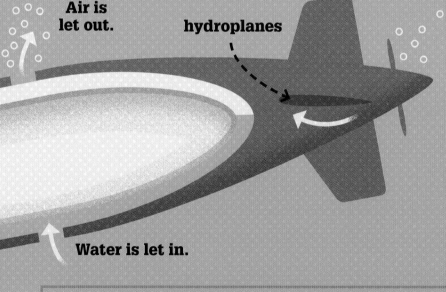

Air is let out.

hydroplanes

Water is let in.

The Russian Typhoon Class submarine is the largest submarine ever built. It is 574 feet (175 m) long, which is more than 2.5 times the wingspan of a jumbo jet.

TRY THIS...

Get two glasses of water, an orange with a peel, and an unpeeled orange. Put one orange in each glass. Which one floats? Why do you think this orange is more buoyant than the other? Go online to see if you are right!

HOW A HOVERCRAFT FLIES

A hovercraft is a special form of transportation that can move easily over land and water. It does this by "flying" on a layer of trapped air.

The Russian Zubr hovercraft is the largest in the world. It can zoom along at more than 60 miles an hour (100 km/h) and carry a load of 165 tons (150 metric tons).

❶ FANS

On the hovercraft are special fans, which push air down under the vehicle.

Air is forced in.

❷ SKIRT

A large rubber skirt around the base of the vehicle traps the air and stops it from escaping.

❸ RISING

As more air is pushed in, the pressure inside the skirt increases, pushing up against the hovercraft until it starts to float or fly above the water.

fan

air

cushion of air

Place a sheet of paper on a tabletop and blow underneath. See how the paper rises up on a cushion of air, just like a hovercraft.

④ PROPELLERS

Propellers on top of the hovercraft are used to push the hovercraft forwards and to steer it.

land

propeller

⑤ FLYING

Because the hovercraft floats above the surface, it can move from water to land quickly and easily.

rubber skirt

The fastest speed ever reached on a hovercraft was 85 miles an hour (137 km/h).

GLOSSARY

AUGER
A screw-shaped device which spins around and moves objects.

AXLE
A rod on which a wheel or a pair of wheels spins around.

BALLAST TANK
A compartment which can be filled with water to make a submarine dive down into the sea.

BORING
Producing a hole or tunnel by using a drill.

CALIPER
A device that uses two movable arms that rotate around a central hinge. The arms on caliper brakes squeeze together on a wheel to slow its spinning.

CHAFF
The unwanted part of a crop.

CHEMICAL ENERGY
Energy stored in chemical form, such as in gasoline, batteries and food, which can be converted into energy.

COG
A wheel with teeth around its edges which transmits forces.

DOWEL
A wooden or metal peg.

DRAGSTER
A type of racing car that competes over straight racetracks.

DRIVE SHAFT
The part of a motor vehicle which transmits force to the wheels.

ELECTRIC CURRENT
A flow of electric charge around a circuit.

ELECTRIC MOTOR
A type of motor which uses the flow of an electric current within a magnetic field to produce movement.

ELEMENT
The part of an electrical device that glows or gets warm when an electric current flows through it.

EXHAUST GASES
The unwanted gases produced by burning fuel inside a gasoline engine.

FRICTION
The force produced when two objects rub past each other.

GEAR
A toothed wheel that transmits a force.

GOUGE
To forcefully scoop something out.

HYDRAULICS
Using liquids to transmit a force.

HYDROELECTRIC DAM

A large wall that blocks the flow of a river and then channels the water it traps through turbines to generate electricity.

LIFT

The force that raises an aircraft up into the air.

MACHINE

A device which alters the power or direction of a force. There are six simple machines: a lever, a wedge, a wheel and axle, a pulley, an inclined plane and a screw.

MOTOR

A device which converts one form of energy, such as the chemical energy in fuel, into movement.

NEWTON

The unit used to measure force.

PISTON

A disc or rod that moves up and down in a cylinder inside an engine.

SPARK PLUG

The part of an engine that produces a spark to set fire to a mixture of air and fuel. This produces the force that drives the engine.

THRESHING DRUM

The part of a combine harvester that separates the grain from the stalks.

THRUST

The force which drives a vehicle forwards.

TRANSFORMER

A device that alters the voltage of an electric current, making it safe to use in our homes.

TURBINE

A wheel that is made up of a number of blades and is sent spinning when a gas or a liquid flows past it.

VALVE

A device which controls the flow of a gas or a liquid.

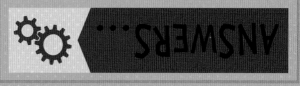

22-23 It would take the train 37 minutes to travel the length of the Seikan Tunnel.

20-21 It would take 17 combine harvesters to harvest the whole field in one day.

16-17 Turbines can be sent spinning using steam or flowing fluid. A hydroelectric dam generates electricity through the gravitational force of flowing water.

12-13 The excavator would need to unload its scoop 20 times to fill the dump truck.

6-7 You will find it easier to cycle up a hill using a low gear.

ANSWERS...

INDEX

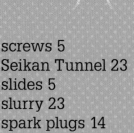

WEBSITES

ny.pbslearningmedia.org/resource/idptv11.
sci.phys.maf.d4ksim/simple-machines/#.
WS2uMxPytVI
Watch this cool video all about simple machines.

easyscienceforkids.com/all-about-simple
-machines/
Learn about technology and machines at this
interactive site.